Death Comes to the Circus

Jan Carew

Stanley Thornes (Publishers) Ltd

© Jan Carew

All rights reserved. No part of this publication may be reproduced or transmitted in any form or by any means, electronic or mechanical, including photocopy, recording, or any information storage and retrieval system, without permission in writing from the publisher or under licence from the Copyright Licensing Agency Limited. Further details of such licences (for reprographic reproduction) may be obtained from the Copyright Licensing Agency Limited, of 90 Tottenham Court Road, London W1P 9HE.

Originally published in 1983 by Hutchinson Education

Reprinted in 1990 by
Stanley Thornes (Publishers) Ltd
Ellenborough House
Wellington Street
CHELTENHAM GL50 1YW

97 98 99 00 / 20 19 18 17 16 15 14 13 12 11

British Library Cataloguing in Publication Data

Carew, Jan
    Death comes to the circus.—(Spirals).
    1. English Language—Readers
    I. Title
    823'.914[J] P27

ISBN 0 7487 0377 2

Cover photo by Zefa
Cover design by Ned Hoste

Set in IBM Pyramid
Printed and bound in Great Britain
Martin's The Printers, Berwick.

1

The fortune-teller was called Madame Bardo. She looked down at the cards in front of her. Under her make-up her face was pale. She hated times like this. That was the trouble with telling fortunes. Sometimes you saw things you didn't want to see.

Quickly, Madame Bardo picked up the cards, and shuffled the pack. She smiled at the two girls sitting across the table. Maria and Gina Donetti were twin sisters. They both had the same dark, curly hair and large brown eyes, the same bright faces full of life. Gina was tired of waiting and her voice was a little sharp. 'Well, come on! What are you waiting for? What do you see in the future?'

Maria was more patient than her sister was. 'Give her a chance, Gina. She has to read the cards first and it takes time.'

Madame Bardo smiled at Maria. 'It's all right. I can tell you some of the future, anyway. You first, Maria.'

Gina frowned, but said nothing. Madame Bardo picked her words with care. She would tell the truth as far as she could. She would just not tell the whole truth.

'I see a stranger coming into your life,' she said. 'A good-looking stranger from abroad. This person will mean a lot to you, Maria. I see love in your future.'

Maria was happy and excited. 'That must be Bruno!' she thought. 'Our cousin Bruno, from Rome. He's coming soon to join our act. He's in one of the best trapeze acts in Italy.'

Gina was tired of waiting for her turn. She didn't want to hear about Maria. She wanted to hear about herself. 'Now, what about my future?' she said. Both her eyes and voice were eager. Madame Bardo didn't really care for Gina but she smiled again.

'Well, Gina,' she said. 'I see a bright future for you as a trapeze artist. You'll be a star one day soon. Everyone will admire you.' Gina's face broke into a smile. This was the kind of thing she wanted to hear. But it wasn't enough.

'What about love?' she asked. 'Do you see any romance for me, like Maria?'

This was a hard question. Madame Bardo wasn't sure what to say. 'Well, I do and I don't. I can't see clearly yet. Perhaps I'm too tired.'

Gina frowned. Then she smiled again. 'But you're sure I'll be a star? You're sure about that?'

'Yes,' said Madame Bardo. 'I'm sure.'

The twins left the caravan and almost bumped into someone on the way. It was Rudy Bardo, the fortune-teller's son. He was a strong lad of seventeen. One of his jobs was to look after the big top and all the ropes and safety nets. Fliers like Maria and Gina depended on the net for their lives.

Rudy smiled at the pretty twins as he went up the steps of the caravan. He never could tell them apart.

His mother was still at the table. There were some cards in front of her. She had tried once more to read the twins' future. She'd hoped the answer would be different.

But it was no use. The cards still gave the same message. Rudy saw his mother's face. It looked sad and tired. 'What is it, mother? What do you see?' asked Rudy.

His mother didn't speak. She picked up the cards quickly. She didn't want Rudy to see one of the cards. It kept coming up, again and again. Every time she read the twins' fortunes.

That card was now hidden at the bottom of the pack. It was the ace of spades — the death card.

2

A few weeks later, Bruno arrived. Both girls liked him from the beginning. He was easy to like, with his dark good looks and his easy laugh. He was a very kind person, too. He wanted to teach the girls all he knew about flying. And he knew a lot.

They began to work on a new act. Bruno wanted both girls to practise a new trick. It was a triple somersault in the air. Both Gina and Maria could already do a double somersault. But a triple one — that was hard. Only the best fliers in the world could do it.

The triple turn needed perfect timing. One moment too soon or too late, and you missed being caught. One day they were to practise the new trick. Gina went to the big top in her blue costume. Maria was always in red, and Bruno in white. The three colours looked good from the ground — red, white and blue.

Gina was a few minutes late and the other two were already there. She could hear their voices from high above. She looked up.

High above the safety net, Bruno hung upside down. His strong legs were curled over the bar. He clapped his hands as a signal to Maria. 'Come on Maria!' called Bruno. 'You'll do it this time!'

Maria stood for a moment on the narrow platform. She seemed a little bit scared. Then she took hold of her trapeze and swung out. One swing, two, three. The third swing took her very high in the air.

Bruno clapped again. That was to tell Maria to let go. Maria was afraid, but she trusted Bruno. She let go and curled her body into a tight ball. Over and over she turned in the air. One, two, three turns — she'd done it!

Now came the hard part. Would Bruno catch her? Or would they miss, as before?

Maria came out of her third turn and Bruno's hands were waiting and ready. His timing had to be perfect also. Gina held her breath, and watched. Maria's body flew through the air like a red arrow. She went straight towards Bruno's hands. Their hands met and grasped. Maria had done it!

3

There was a little cheer from the crowd. Some of the circus people were watching too. Two of the clowns were there and also Rudy Bardo.

'Well done, Maria! Well done, Bruno!' called one of the clowns.

Maria flew back to the platform and landed. She looked down and saw her sister.

'Gina!' she called. 'Come up, Gina! Come and try the triple.'

Gina went up the rope quickly. Like all trapeze artists, she could climb like a cat.

Bruno told Gina what to do. He wanted her to try the trick as well. Gina listened hard. She hoped she could do the trick as well as Maria. Perhaps even better.

At the clap from Bruno, Gina swung out. One, two, three swings. Bruno clapped again. That was when Gina ought to let go. But somehow she couldn't. She was afraid, and clung to the bar for a few seconds.

Then she let go and began to turn over. But she didn't reach the third turn. And she was too low in the air for Bruno to catch her. She missed his hands and felt herself fall. Down, down, down.

She bounced in the safety net, her legs and arms stuck up in the air. She looked quite a comical sight and a few people laughed. Gina hated them for it.

'Come on, Gina! Try again!' Bruno called from above. 'Maria had to try it lots of times. Come on!'

But Gina wouldn't.

Next day, they had another try at the triple turn. This time Gina did manage it, but only once. The other five times she fell in the net. Maria was much better at it. So Bruno decided that Maria would do the triple and Gina would catch her.

Gina didn't say much, but she felt angry. Maria always seemed to be in the lime-light. And she was sure Bruno loved her sister. She could see the way he looked at her. Maria always seemed to have everything.

Why should Maria have Bruno's love and not her? Why should everyone like Maria and not her? Why should Maria be the star of the show and not her? It wasn't fair. Besides, if she changed places with Maria, no-one would even notice.

4

One night, they all stood in the shadows, waiting to begin their act. The big top was filled with white light and the sound of laughter. The clowns were on.

Then the ring was empty and the band started the music for the trapeze act. A spotlight swung round to the three waiting figures. The red, white and blue costumes shone in the light. Bruno took each of the girls by the hand. They walked forward into the circle of light. The light made it hard to see. The crowd became a sea of faces. A loud cheer came from the crowd. The trapeze act was one of the best in the circus.

They all took a rope and were pulled up to the two platforms on either side of the ring. The trapeze bars hung ready.

Then the band played 'The Blue Danube' waltz and the act began. Back and forwards flew the red, white and blue figures. The act went like clockwork. Bruno did a' lot of the catching. The girls seemed to fly through the air like swallows to his hands. Then the act became more daring. Bruno, Gina and Maria all did a double somersault in turn, and were caught.

Then came the high point of the act. The crowd held its breath. What next?

It was time for the triple turn. Bruno watched and could hardly believe his eyes. The girls had changed places! Maria, in her red costume, hung upside down in the centre of the ring. Her hands were ready and waiting to catch. He looked across at the other platform. He saw a shining blue figure, ready to swing out.

What the hell were the girls playing at? Gina wasn't ready to do the triple turn yet. She would make a mess of it. He tried to call out 'No, Gina! Don't go!' But it was too late.

The blue figure swung out on the trapeze. With a dry mouth, Bruno watched. One, two, three swings. Up high in the air. Once, twice, three times! She'd done it! Gina had done it after all!

Bruno was about to cheer. Then he caught his breath in horror. Something had gone wrong. Somehow, the blue figure and the red one missed each other. It was all over in a second. One moment, they seemed to grasp hands; the next, they were apart. The blue figure fell away into space.

Bruno didn't panic. There was no need to. The

safety net was there. He watched as the slim blue form fell down into the net.

Then something happened which he could not believe. The safety net gave way! It fell slowly to the ground.

But not slowly enough. The body of the girl in blue lay in a strange way. Her neck was broken by the fall.

5

It was a terrible thing for the circus. Everyone was deeply upset by Gina's death. It was worst of all for Rudy Bardo. He felt that the accident must be his fault. The safety net was one of his jobs. He couldn't understand how it had broken. Unless — someone had made it loose. But that couldn't be true. No-one would do a thing like that. No, he'd better face the truth. He must have been careless.

The trapeze act would have to be changed. There were only two of them — Bruno and Maria. Maria was the star. She had to do the triple somersault and be caught by Bruno. They practised hard. But Bruno felt that something was strange. Maria wasn't as good as she used to be. Perhaps Gina's accident had made her afraid. That must be it, thought Bruno.

So he was very kind to Maria. He worked very hard to help her get back her old skill. The triple turn was still to be the high point of the act.

But Maria didn't seem the same girl at all. In other ways as well. She didn't seem such a warm person as before. It must be Gina's death, thought Bruno. After all, they were twins.

He didn't feel so close to Maria now. She was so

strange and jumpy. Her nerves must be bad, thought Bruno.

One day, he came to collect her from her caravan. They were due to practise in the big top. Maria wasn't dressed yet, however. She was standing at the door of her caravan, holding her red costume in her hand and looking very angry. Before her stood a small group of circus people. The wardrobe lady was there and Maria was shouting at her.

'Don't tell me it's just come from the cleaners,' said Maria. 'I don't believe it. It doesn't even smell fresh, let alone look it.' Certainly, the costume did look as if it had been worn. Bruno thought so, too. Then one of the circus people spoke. It was one of the clowns. 'But Maria,' he said. 'You wore it this afternoon. Don't you remember? We met outside the big top. You were in your red costume then. So of course it's been worn.'

The wardrobe lady was quite cross. 'Well, I never!' she said. 'Blaming me like that! If I say a thing is clean, it is clean. Be more careful next time, young lady.' And she walked off in a huff.

The other people went off too and left Bruno and Maria alone. Bruno didn't quite know what to say. Maria's anger seemed to have gone suddenly. She stood holding the costume up to her cheek, and her dark eyes met Bruno's. Bruno couldn't be sure, but he thought he saw fear in those eyes.

Maria spoke but her words didn't make sense to Bruno. She seemed to be talking to herself. 'But it's not my scent,' she said softly, holding the costume near to her face. 'It's not my scent.'

6

Bruno almost forgot about Maria's strange words in the next few weeks. He went on working hard with Maria in the ring. And it paid off. She seemed to get back all her old skill and relax more. It was almost like before Gina's accident. Almost, but not quite. There was something different, but Bruno couldn't put his finger on it.

Then, one day he got a terrible fright. He was walking towards the big top for his usual practice. Burt Kelly, the lion-tamer, had warned him to take the long way round. Burt was going to change the animals' cages that day. So no-one was to take the usual shortcut past the lions' cages. Everyone had been warned. At least, so Bruno thought. Suddenly, there was a scream, and Bruno's heart nearly stopped. It was Maria's voice. He was sure of it. And it came from the lions' cages! Quickly, Bruno ran towards them. He soon saw Maria. She was unable to move for fear. And there was a large lion about four feet from her. It looked at the girl with its big yellow eyes. Then its mouth opened and it snarled, showing huge teeth. Bruno's mouth felt as dry as paper. It could all be over in a few seconds. He knew that. Once that lion decided to spring, there'd be no way to save Maria. She'd be torn to pieces. He looked round for a bit of wood or a stick. Something to use against the lion. But he couldn't see anything.

The lion scraped the ground with its paws and made claw marks in the dust. It was getting ready to spring.

Then a man's voice was heard. 'Get back, Simba! Get back, I say!' It was the lion-tamer, Burt Kelly. He cracked his whip and shouted at the animal. Slowly, it moved back, and went into an empty cage. Burt Kelly ran forward and shut the door.

Maria was almost sick with fear. Her breath came in huge gasps. Bruno ran forward and put his arm around her. But Maria paid no attention to Bruno. She was looking at Burt Kelly and her eyes blazed with anger.

'What do you mean by letting that animal run loose? I could have been killed! I'll see you get into trouble for this!'

But Burt Kelly was angry, too. 'Now just a minute, Maria,' he said. 'You can't say I didn't warn you. I told you to stay away from here today. I told everyone to use the other path. I have to change the cages today. But I told you this morning. How could you forget?'

But Maria wouldn't listen. 'What are you talking about?' she shouted. 'You didn't tell me anything about it. You're only trying to cover up. You and your horrible animals! I'll see you pay for this!' And she went off in a temper.

Bruno looked at Burt Kelly. He didn't know what to think. Burt wasn't usually a liar. And he didn't take risks. If he was sure he'd told Maria, then it must be true. So why didn't Maria remember?

Bruno felt very worried about Maria. This wasn't the first time she had behaved strangely. Could she be having black-outs? Doing things and then forgetting she'd done them? There was something wrong with Maria. She was so nervy and jumpy. Bruno wished he knew what was wrong.

7

One night, Bruno passed Maria's caravan. He decided to call in on her to see how she was. The show was long since over, and most people had gone to bed. But for some reason, Bruno felt uneasy. He didn't feel like going to bed yet.

He was about to knock at the door when he heard Maria's voice. It came from inside the caravan through the open window. The words didn't make sense to Bruno. And yet, he felt a chill near his heart in spite of the warm summer night.

'Go away!' said Maria's voice. 'Go away! You're dead. I killed you, Maria. I'm not afraid of you. The dead can't harm the living. Go away!' Bruno could just make out the girl's face through the window. She was talking to a mirror on the wall.

And in that moment, Bruno began to understand. At last. All sorts of little things clicked into place in his mind. The way Maria seemed so different to him after the accident. Her old warmth seemed to have gone. There was a sharper note in her voice. Also, her skill on the trapeze seemed to be lost after Gina's death. All kinds of things began to make sense.

The girl he flew with in the ring every night was not Maria at all. It was Gina. Bruno felt sure of it. It explained so many things.

Bruno thought back to that dreadful night six months ago. The night of the accident on the trapeze. He forced himself to remember what had happened. He saw it all happen again in his mind.

A slim blue form swung out to do the triple turn. A red form swung in the centre, ready to catch her. Bruno, like everyone else, thought it was Gina who swung out to her death. But the girls could have changed costumes! It was possible. In that case, it was *Maria* who fell from the trapeze.

Bruno felt sure he was right. It was such a simple thing, to know someone by the colour of their costume. He had never thought to question it before.

But there was something far worse. Bruno was sure of something else now. The fall that night was no accident. It was planned. Why did the girls' hands meet and then part? And above all, why did the safety net collapse? It had never done so before. Someone must have loosened the ropes.

And Bruno knew who that someone was. He was sure it was Gina. His partner — a murderer.

8

Bruno crept quietly away from the caravan and went home. He slept badly that night, torn by nightmares. Thoughts and memories rushed through his mind. He blamed himself for not seeing the truth sooner. He ought to have guessed. And yet, how could he? It was too horrible.

He didn't know what to do. He ought to tell someone what he thought. But he had no proof. It was very difficult. Bruno decided to wait for a little while. He would think of what to do.

He tried to behave as usual with his partner in the ring. But he avoided her eyes when they were on the ground. He couldn't bear her to touch him, even by accident.

One evening after the show, the two of them walked home together. It was a lovely night and the caravans were silver shapes in the moonlight. Bruno felt his partner's arm slip into his and her warm body lean against him.

'Oh Bruno,' she murmured. 'What a lovely night. Don't you think so?'

Her face turned up towards him, as if she expected

him to kiss her. Bruno just couldn't bring himself to do it. He knew it was dangerous not to, but he couldn't help it.

He heard the sharp hiss as she caught her breath and looked straight into his eyes. Bruno felt helpless to hide what he felt. The girl looked at Bruno for a full minute, and then turned and walked away.

Bruno didn't know how much she read in his eyes. But, for some reason, he was afraid.

9

He didn't see much of his partner after that night. Only in the ring. They went through their act every night and hardly spoke at other times. Bruno didn't know what Gina was thinking. But there was a cold glint in her eyes sometimes. It sent a shiver through Bruno.

One night before the show, Bruno found a message in his caravan. It was written in capital letters and looked very urgent.

'MEET ME AT ABDUL'S CARAVAN. COME AT ONCE.'

It was signed by the circus boss.

Bruno didn't stop to wonder about the message. It was clear he had to go at once.

Abdul, the snake-charmer, lived on the other side of the field from Bruno. His snake act was just after the trapeze one. Perhaps there was some problem about that. Maybe the boss wanted to change the order of the acts.

Bruno walked quickly round to Abdul's caravan. It was beginning to get darker. The nights were drawing in now and there was a slight nip in the air. Soon summer would be over and the circus would pack up and move on.

Abdul's caravan was lit up but no-one answered Bruno's knock. That was strange. Where was the boss? Where was Abdul? Maybe they hadn't come yet.

Bruno tried the handle of the door and it opened. He might as well go inside. It would be warmer. He could wait for the others in there.

Bruno went across to a sofa and sat down to wait. A few minutes passed, and then Bruno began to feel the hair rise on the back of his neck. He felt he wasn't alone.

There was a soft sound near him. A gentle creak, like something moving in a basket. Bruno could hear a slithery sound as it moved. It was something with scaly skin.

Bruno wasn't a coward by nature. Very few things could scare him. But he had one great horror, and it was snakes. He could not stand them.

He didn't want to make a sudden move, so he turned his head only. Towards that sound. A cry rose in his throat but didn't come out. There was a large snake. Bruno thought it was a python. He wasn't sure. He didn't care. Frozen with terror, he saw the snake's head sway back and forth. Its cold eyes gleamed at him. It moved slowly out of its basket, and crawled towards him. It was between him and the door.

10

Suddenly, the door burst open. It was Abdul, the snake-charmer. He took in the scene at one glance. He saw Bruno, unable to move on the sofa. He also saw the snake.

Quickly and expertly, Abdul got the snake back into its basket. He put the catch on the lid, and turned to Bruno.

'That was a near thing,' he said. 'The snakes know me, but to a stranger they can be dangerous. What made you come here, Bruno?'

Bruno showed Abdul the note. The snake-charmer looked at it silently.

'That is strange,' he said. 'I got a message tonight, also. I was getting the snakes ready for tonight's show. I always handle them before the act. It makes them easier to handle in the ring. But this note came through my door. Look.'

And he showed Bruno a message. It was also written in block letters.

'COME TO MY CARAVAN AT ONCE.'

It was signed by the boss, just like Bruno's note.

'The boss knew nothing about it,' said Abdul. 'It was a hoax. But on my way back, I met Maria.'

'Maria?' asked Bruno. His voice was faint. He was still suffering from shock.

'Yes,' said Abdul. 'She was very excited. She told me you were in danger. I was to get back here at once. And she was right. I was just in time.'

'Yes,' said Bruno. 'I was never so glad to see anyone. Thanks, Abdul. I'd better get back now. The show begins soon.'

Abdul looked at Bruno's pale face. 'Are you all right to go on tonight, Bruno? You don't look well.'

Bruno tried to smile. 'I'm OK,' he said. 'I just don't like snakes, that's all. I'll be fine.'

Abdul smiled too, but his eyes were worried.

'Take care, then, Bruno. I don't like what happened tonight. Someone sent those false messages. You seem to have an enemy in the circus. Take care tonight on the trapeze.'

11

Bruno walked back home with Abdul's words ringing in his ears. 'You have an enemy in the circus. Take care tonight on the trapeze.'

Bruno's lips set tight.

'I'm more at home in the air than on the ground,' he thought. 'I'll be all right on the trapeze. It's other times I'm worried about.'

It wasn't a good feeling to have. Knowing someone wanted you dead. Someone who would stop at nothing. Someone who had killed already.

'It's Gina,' thought Bruno. 'She knows I've guessed her secret. She wants me out of the way. Then she'll be safe.'

But who had told Abdul that Bruno was in danger from the snake? Not Gina, that was certain. Gina had very likely written the notes and set the trap.

Bruno frowned and thought hard as he walked. Abdul said that Maria had told him about Bruno's danger. Suppose that was true? Suppose the real Maria had come back? Bruno didn't believe in ghosts and yet — other strange things had happened lately. Things he couldn't understand.

For instance, there was the row about the red costume. Someone had worn it and his partner swore she hadn't. Then there was the time the lion nearly killed Gina. She said then that no-one had told her about the cages being opened. But Burt Kelly was sure he had told her. So he must have told someone.

It was all very strange. Bruno also remembered the time he overheard Gina talking to the mirror. That was when he first knew the truth. He thought Gina was haunted by her sister's memory because she was guilty. Suppose it was more than that? Suppose Maria's ghost really had come back?

12

Suddenly, Bruno felt that he was no longer alone. Someone was walking beside him. It was a girl and her feet made no noise on the wet grass. She had appeared so quickly that Bruno hadn't seen her come.

The slim form was very well known to Bruno. So was the pretty face with dark eyes, softly lit by the lamps from the caravans. A faint scent reached Bruno. It was flowery and it awoke memories in him.

'Maria,' he whispered, hardly daring to say the name. Her voice came softly on the night air. 'Yes Bruno. It is Maria. You know the truth now, Bruno. You know what my sister did. And what she tried to do to you tonight. She is clever, Bruno. She knows you suspect her and she is out to kill you. I saved you tonight but she will try again. But have no fear, my love. I shall never be far away. You may not see me, but I'll be there.'

Bruno opened his mouth to speak but there was nobody there. Had he dreamed it all? Bruno had no way of knowing.

Suddenly, the music from the big top broke into

Bruno's thoughts. It would soon be time for the trapeze act. He had better hurry up.

Then he remembered something with a sick feeling in the pit of his stomach. Tonight, he and Gina had to fly without the safety net. It was to attract bigger crowds. Bruno hated the idea but he had to agree. It was the boss's idea. Things had got quiet lately and not many people came to the circus. The boss had dropped hints about getting rid of some acts, even closing down if things got too bad. So Bruno didn't have much choice.

However, there was no real reason to worry. Tonight, there would be no triple turn. It was much too dangerous without a net. Also, Gina was doing no catching tonight, so Bruno could relax. He would be quite safe.

13

A little while later, Bruno and Gina waited for their entrance music. There was a big crowd tonight. You could tell by the noise. Word had got round about the safety net being taken down. People love a thrill like that.

The two fliers walked out into the spotlight and bowed to the cheering crowd. Then they climbed up their ropes to the little platforms high above. The crowd grew quiet and looked up. They could see the two shapes a long way up. One red and one white. The waltz music began and the couple went into their act.

They did very simple tricks at first. It was quite easy for them. But it looked good from below. And it looked very risky without a net.

Bruno began to relax. Soon the trapeze act would be over. Surely nothing could go wrong now.

When something did, it took Bruno completely by surprise. He was doing one of his last tricks — a very easy one. He did it every night and hardly had to think about it. He had to fly out on one bar, let go in the air, and then grab another bar.

The second bar was only used by Bruno for this special trick.

It was when his fingers reached out to grasp the second bar that he noticed something odd. The bar had a strange shine about it. It should be dry but it was wet and slippery. There was oil on the bar.

Bruno's eyes saw this fact, but too late to help him. He had already let go the first bar. He was in mid-air and his hands reached out towards that softly gleaming bar. His fingers grabbed, slipped, grabbed again. But he had no chance of holding on. No-one could have.

Bruno started to fall.

14

The crowd below gasped in horror. Below Bruno there was nothing but space. What could save him now?

As he began to fall, Bruno's hands reached out and clawed at the air. But he had no real hope.

Suddenly, a trapeze bar swung towards him. It was as if a wind had moved it. Bruno caught it with one hand, and hung for a moment. Then he had both hands firmly on the bar. He was safe!

The crowd breathed again and broke into a cheer. They didn't know what had happened so far above. It was all over in a moment. But they didn't care. The main thing was, the danger was past.

Bruno flew back to his platform and landed. His heart thudded loudly like a drum and his throat was dry with fear. He had never been so close to death and he knew it. He also knew who had saved him. That meeting with Maria tonight — he hadn't dreamed it after all.

Bruno got ready to slide down his rope. His legs shook a little but he knew he'd be all right now. Again Gina had done her worst and again she'd failed.

He looked across the ring at his partner. The girl in red made no move to come down. She was staring out into space. As if she couldn't believe what she saw. But what was she staring at? There was nothing to see. Only an empty trapeze in the centre of the ring.

Suddenly, the girl moved. She took her own trapeze in her hands and got ready to swing out.

'What is she doing?' Bruno asked himself.

The crowd went very quiet. They also felt that something was wrong. High above, they saw a red figure swing out on a bar.

The red figure let go of the bar and flew into space. She curled up and turned a somersault. Once, twice, three times. The third turn took her near the empty bar in the centre. The bar she had been staring at.

Her hands went out. As if to a waiting catcher. That was the greatest horror of all. She seemed to think someone was there!

And then she fell.

A great groan rose from the crowd. But it didn't hide the dull thud of the girl's body on the ground.

Circus people ran out into the ring. They stood round the girl's broken body, and hid it from the crowd. All eyes were fixed on the ground at that moment.

Bruno clung to his rope high above on the platform. A wave of sickness hit him. He tried to get his head clear. He closed his eyes and then opened them. And he saw something no-one else did.

In the middle of the ring was the empty trapeze. No-one had used it. And yet, it swung gently to and fro.